THE GREAT BOOKS FOUN

Discussion Guide *for Teachers*

# THE HARLEM RENAISSANCE

## About Perfection Learning

Founded by two educators, Perfection Learning is a family-owned company that has provided innovative, effective reading, literature, and language arts materials to K–12 classroom teachers for more than eighty-five years. Through the design of its literature programs and its partnership with the Great Books Foundation, the company offers two flagship literature programs, Many Voices and Literature & Thought, each of which focus using engaging, thought-provoking literature selections to teach middle and high school students to be critical readers and thinkers. Each anthology is structured to help students explore essential questions and develop the skills necessary to be successful in the 21st century.

## About the Great Books Foundation

The Great Books Foundation is an independent, nonprofit educational organization that works toward a sustainable and just democracy. We create reading and discussion programs for students and adults with the conviction that literacy and critical thinking help develop reflective and well-informed citizens. We believe that civil and open discussion of the world's enduring literature promotes empathy, understanding, and community, and that by working to develop reading and thinking skills, we advance the ultimate promise of democracy—participation for all.

The Great Books Foundation was established in 1947 to promote liberal education for the general public. In 1962, Great Books extended its mission to children with the introduction of Junior Great Books®. Since its inception, Great Books has helped thousands of people throughout the United States and in other countries begin their own discussion groups in schools, libraries, and community centers. Today, Great Books instructors conduct hundreds of professional development courses for teachers and parents each year, and Great Books programs help more than one million students learn to read, discuss, and appreciate some of the world's most enduring literature.

THE GREAT BOOKS FOUNDATION

# Discussion Guide *for* Teachers

# THE HARLEM RENAISSANCE

Perfection Learning

∼

**Great**
**Books**
Foundation

10  11  12  PP  19  18  17
Printed in the United States of America

Published and distributed by

**The Great Books Foundation**
*A nonprofit educational organization*

233 North Michigan Avenue, Suite 420
Chicago, IL 60601
www.greatbooks.org

# CONTENTS

# INTRODUCTION

This discussion guide for *The Harlem Renaissance* focuses on several selections that the Great Books Foundation recommends for close reading and discussion using the Foundation's Shared Inquiry™ method. This collaborative, inquiry-based process complements the critical thinking encouraged by Perfection Learning's *Literature & Thought* series, and will inform your students' thinking about the essential question, "What was the Harlem Renaissance?" posed at the beginning of the book.

Shared Inquiry is the effort to achieve a better understanding of a text by discussing questions, responses, and insights with others. For both the leader and the participants, careful listening is essential. The leader guides the discussion by asking questions about specific ideas and problems of meaning in the text, but does not seek to impose his or her own interpretation on the group. To be an effective leader of Shared Inquiry Discussion, training from the Great Books Foundation is strongly recommended.

The Great Books Foundation offers a range of professional development opportunities for discussion leaders, including an introductory two-day workshop and advanced workshops in the practice of Shared Inquiry. Participants learn how to frame questions that genuinely engage students, use follow-up questions to explore students' ideas more thoughtfully, and involve students of all abilities in focused, lively discussions. Instructors from the Foundation are also available for follow-up consultation days, which include classroom demonstrations and coaching. For more information, call the Foundation at 1-800-222-5870 or visit our Web site at www.greatbooks.org.

The Shared Inquiry approach develops students' reading comprehension in the context of thinking about genuine problems of meaning raised by a selection. The interpretive activities suggested in this Discussion Guide are designed to help students become more aware of their reactions as they read, develop a sensitivity to language, and value their own curiosity about a text. The focus on interpretation and discussion means that all students can participate confidently and improve their abilities to read and think critically about literature.

# Your Role
## as Leader

As the discussion leader, you serve as a model of an involved, curious thinker. By asking open-ended questions and showing genuine interest in your students' ideas, you help everyone reach a greater understanding of the selection.

We recommend that you prepare for each discussion unit by reading the selection closely and noting your own reactions and questions. Your preparation is as important as that of your students; knowing the selection well enables you to lead effectively. During your second reading, you may wish to mark the selection using the suggested note-taking prompt. These preparatory steps will help you consider the interpretive issues that the selection raises and plan your class schedule of activities.

# Sample Schedules
## of Activities

In-class work on a Great Books discussion unit consists of

- Reading the selection aloud and identifying questions worth exploring (Sharing Questions)

- Rereading the selection, taking notes (Directed Notes), and comparing those notes with others

- Shared Inquiry Discussion, the culminating activity in which interpretive questions are explored in depth

The activities that precede discussion—the Text Opener, reading the selection aloud, Sharing Questions, and a second reading with Directed Notes—will help students think for themselves about the selection and prepare them to develop their own interpretations in discussion. Most teachers will want to extend this process with the suggested Writing After Discussion activities, which encourage further reflection on the issues raised by the selection and give students the opportunity to synthesize and elaborate on their ideas, making them relevant to their own lives.

Following are two sample weekly schedules. The length of the in-class sessions will vary according to the length of the selection. Depending on your students' needs, you may choose to assign some activities as homework.

## Option A: Three In-class Sessions

### Session 1

- Text Opener *(optional)*
- First reading of the selection
- Sharing Questions

### Session 2

- Second reading with Directed Notes
- Comparing and discussing notes

### Session 3

- Shared Inquiry Discussion

**Homework:** Writing After Discussion *(optional)*


## Option B: Two In-class Sessions

### Session 1

- First reading of the selection
- Sharing Questions

**Homework:** Second reading with Directed Notes

### Session 2

- Comparing and discussing notes
- Shared Inquiry Discussion

**Homework:** Writing After Discussion *(optional)*

# CONDUCTING THE
# INTERPRETIVE ACTIVITIES

**Text Opener:** 10–20 minutes *(optional)*

- Sparks students' interest in the selection by introducing a theme or issue they will encounter in the text

- Helps students connect their own experiences to the text

Before the first reading, you may choose to conduct the Text Opener with students, particularly if the selection is likely to prove challenging or foreign to them. A short discussion of students' responses is sufficient, since the goal is to spur their interest in reading the selection. You may wish to have students write briefly (for no more than five minutes) before discussing their responses.

**First Reading:** 10–15 minutes *(depends on selection length)*

- Allows students to enjoy the story

- Helps students take in unfamiliar vocabulary

- Gives students the model of a fluent reader using appropriate pace and expression

- Ensures that all students begin their interpretive work on an equal footing

- Leads naturally to students sharing questions about the selection

We recommend reading the selection aloud to your students as they follow along in their books and note questions that occur to them.

## Sharing Questions: 15–20 minutes

- Teaches students that their curiosity and desire to know are starting points for interpretive thinking

- Develops the habit of reflecting and questioning after reading

- Clears up initial misreadings and comprehension difficulties

- Generates questions worth exploring in discussion

- Fosters a cooperative atmosphere in which students are comfortable raising questions to explore with the group

After the first reading, ask for students' initial reactions to the selection *(What did you think? How did you like it?)*, then encourage them to ask any questions they have about the selection, including vocabulary questions (see p. 25). You should briefly consider possible answers to students' questions and clear up any issues that interfere with comprehension, while identifying other questions to be considered further in discussion. We recommend that you write down students' questions, perhaps posting them on the board or on chart paper for all to see. Looking over students' questions after the session is an excellent way to gauge their curiosity and to plan your discussion of the selection.

## Second Reading with Directed Notes: 25–40 minutes

- Gives students guided practice in deciding which parts of a text require closer examination

- Improves students' ability to recall and use supporting evidence for their opinions

- Helps students draw connections as they read and recognize interpretive issues

- Helps students recognize that a passage can have different interpretations

- Encourages the habit of using notes as a way of reacting to and thinking about literature

Reading twice and taking notes during the second reading are distinctive features of Great Books programs and may be new to students. We recommend that you explain to students the reasons for rereading and note taking: this careful consideration of the text deepens understanding, and written notes offer readers a way to think about, remember, and share their reactions to a story.

Suggested note-taking prompts for each selection highlight interpretive issues in the text. Marking the text according to the prompt makes it easy to compare the reactions of different individuals to the same passage. The following suggestions will help your students get the most out of note taking:

- Allow time for students to discuss some of their notes, so that they see different interpretive possibilities and understand the value of explaining their notes to others.

- Lead a brief discussion of students' notes on one or two pages of the selection, asking students to share not only what they marked but also the thinking behind their notes.

- Ask questions like *Why did you mark the passage that way? Did anyone else mark it that way? Did anyone mark it differently? Why?* to help students understand both their thinking and that of others.

- You may also choose to have students discuss their notes in pairs while you circulate through the room, asking follow-up questions as needed.

Here are examples of how two different students marked the same story when asked to mark places where the main character **accepts** reality with **A**, and places where he **escapes** reality with **E.**

moment fifteen years before when he had told her—innocently—that such a supper tasted "right nice. Kinda change from what we always has."

He mounted the four brick steps leading to his door and pulled at the bell, but there was no answering ring. It was broken again, and in a mental flash he saw himself with a multitude of tools and a box of matches shivering in the vestibule after supper. He began to pound lustily on the door and wondered vaguely if his hand would bleed if he smashed the glass. He hated the sight of blood. It sickened him.

*A knows what is required of him*

Some one was running down the stairs. Daisy probably. Millie would be at that infernal thing, pounding, pounding.... He entered. The chill of the house swept him. His child was wrapped in a coat. She whispered solemnly, "Poppa, Miz Hicks an' Miz Berry's orful mad. They gointa move if they can't get more heat. The furnace's birnt out all day. Mama couldn't fix it." He said hurriedly, "I'll go right down. I'll go right down." He hoped Mrs. Hicks wouldn't pull open her door and glare at him. She was large and domineering, and her husband was a bully. If her husband ever struck him it would kill him. He hated life, but he didn't want to die. He was afraid of God, and in his wildest flights of fancy couldn't imagine himself an angel. He went softly down the stairs.

*A does his duty*

*A is resigned to life*

He began to shake the furnace fiercely. And he shook into it every wrong, mumbling softly under his breath. He began to think back over his uneventful years, and it came to him as rather a shock that he had never sworn in all his life. He wondered uneasily if he dared say "damn." It was taken for granted that a man swore when he tended a stubborn furnace. And his strongest interjection was "Great balls of fire!"

*E wants to break out of his shell*

The cellar began to warm, and he took off his inadequate overcoat that was streaked with dirt. Well, Net would have to clean that. He'd be damned—! It frightened him and thrilled him. He wanted suddenly to rush upstairs and tell Mrs. Hicks if she didn't like the way he was running things, she could get out. But he heaped another shovelful of coal on the fire and sighed. He would never be able to get away from himself and the routine of years.

*E*

He thought of that eager Negro lad of seventeen who had come North to seek his fortune. He had walked jauntily down Boylston Street, and even his own kind had laughed at the incongruity of him. But he

13

moment fifteen years before when he had told her—innocently—
that such a supper tasted "right nice. Kinda change from what we
always has."

(A) He mounted the four brick steps leading to his door and pulled at the
bell, but there was no answering ring. It was broken again, and in a
mental flash he saw himself with a multitude of tools and a box of
matches shivering in the vestibule after supper. He began to pound
lustily on the door and wondered vaguely if his hand would bleed if he
smashed the glass. He hated the sight of blood. It sickened him.

Some one was running down the stairs. Daisy probably. Millie would
be at that infernal thing, pounding, pounding.... He entered. The chill
of the house swept him. His child was wrapped in a coat. She whispered solemnly, "Poppa, Miz Hicks an' Miz Berry's orful mad. They
gointa move if they can't get more heat. The furnace's birnt out all day
(A) Mama couldn't fix it." He said hurriedly, "I'll go right down. I'll go right
down." He hoped Mrs. Hicks wouldn't pull open her door and glare at
him. She was large and domineering, and her husband was a bully. If her
(A) husband ever struck him it would kill him. He hated life, but he didn'
want to die. He was afraid of God, and in his wildest flights of fancy
couldn't imagine himself an angel. He went softly down the stairs.

He began to shake the furnace fiercely. And he shook into it every
wrong, mumbling softly under his breath. He began to think back over
(E) can't his uneventful years, and it came to him as rather a shock that he had
shake the never sworn in all his life. He wondered uneasily if he dared say
people "damn." It was taken for granted that a man swore when he tended
who a stubborn furnace. And his strongest interjection was "Great balls
upset him of fire!"

The cellar began to warm, and he took off his inadequate overcoat
that was streaked with dirt. Well, Net would have to clean that. He'd be
damned—! It frightened him and thrilled him. He wanted suddenly to
rush upstairs and tell Mrs. Hicks if she didn't like the way he was running things, she could get out. But he heaped another shovelful of coal
(A) on the fire and sighed. He would never be able to get away from him-
resigned self and the routine of years.

He thought of that eager Negro lad of seventeen who had come
North to seek his fortune. He had walked jauntily down Boylston Street
and even his own kind had laughed at the incongruity of him. But he

14

## Shared Inquiry Discussion: 30–45 minutes

- Encourages students to present arguments clearly and persuasively, to offer reasons for their opinions and inferences, and to support their ideas with evidence

- Helps students analyze character motivation and development, as well as cause and effect

- Helps students learn to weigh the merits of opposing arguments and to modify their initial opinions

- Gives students the confidence to shape and express their own opinions about what they read

- Gives students practice in active listening and cooperative learning

In this cornerstone activity of Great Books programs, students work together to interpret the text, guided by the open-ended questioning of the leader. We recommend that students be given time to reflect individually on the leader's opening question before discussion begins, so that they can gather their thoughts and examine the text for evidence. Having students write down their answers on the Building Your Answer activity page (pp. 22–23) is an excellent way to begin discussion, and enables you to call on less vocal students knowing that they have something to contribute. The Building Your Answer page also includes a portion for use at the end of discussion, to encourage students to reconsider their initial answers.

While this guide provides discussion questions for each unit, we encourage you to use these in combination with questions generated by you or your students. Focus questions appear in boldface type, followed by a group of related questions; these can be used in any order depending on the progress of the discussion, the needs of your students, and your teaching goals.

## Creating a Good Environment for Shared Inquiry Discussion

Establishing an atmosphere that promotes discussion involves preparing both the classroom and the students themselves.

**Setting up the classroom.** Try to arrange the room so that everyone can see and hear each other. Your students should have a convenient surface on which to place their books and open them up. Ideally, have students sit around a table or arrange their desks in a circle or square. This type of arrangement stimulates discussion and helps students realize that the ideas offered by their classmates can be a major source of insight into a selection. If it isn't possible to arrange the room in this way, encourage students to look at the person talking, acknowledging one another and not just the leader.

**Introducing students to Shared Inquiry.** For some students, it will be a new idea that you will not be providing answers but instead asking open-ended questions with more than one reasonable answer. Emphasize to students that you and they are partners in Shared Inquiry, and that you will be asking questions you care about and need their ideas to resolve. Encourage students to raise questions of their own and to speak to each other rather than always to you.

In addition to explaining how Shared Inquiry Discussion works, it is vital that your students understand the guidelines the class will follow during discussion and the reasons for them. For this purpose, we recommend distributing the handout on the next page before your first discussion.

# Discussion Guidelines

Come to discussion with your book, a pen or pencil, a notebook, and an open mind. In Shared Inquiry Discussion, everyone, including the leader, considers a question with more than one reasonable answer and weighs the evidence for different answers. The goal of discussion is for each of you to develop an answer that satisfies you personally.

Following the rules outlined below will make for a better discussion:

★ **Read the selection before participating in the discussion.** This ensures that all participants are equally prepared to talk about the ideas in the work and helps prevent talk that would distract the group from its purpose.

★ **Support your ideas with evidence from the text.** This keeps the discussion focused on understanding the selection. It will enable the group to weigh textual support for different answers and to choose intelligently among them.

★ **Discuss the ideas in the selection, and try to understand them fully before exploring issues that go beyond the selection.** Weighing evidence for different interpretations is essential before exploring related issues or deciding whether we agree with the author.

★ **Listen to others and respond to them directly.** Shared Inquiry is about the give-and-take of ideas, a willingness to listen to others and to talk to them respectfully. Directing your comments and questions to other group members, not always to the leader, will make the discussion livelier and more dynamic.

★ **Expect the leader to ask questions, rather than answer them.** The leader's role is to keep discussion effective and interesting by listening and asking questions. The leader's goal is to help participants develop their own ideas, with everyone (the leader included) gaining a new understanding in the process.

## Building Your Answer Activity Page

We recommend that before each discussion you distribute copies of the Building Your Answer page (see pp. 22–23) to students. Ask them to take about five minutes to write down their initial thoughts about your opening question before discussion begins. Doing so encourages students to think more deeply about their answers and allows quieter students to frame a response that they will feel confident sharing. After discussion, students can finish their Building Your Answer pages in class or as homework.

## Leading Discussion Effectively

Leading Shared Inquiry Discussion is a process that you can expect to become easier over time. If you lead discussion regularly, both you and your class will grow more confident and comfortable with it. The following suggestions should help you.

**Begin the discussion with a real question.** Ask a question that you are genuinely struggling to answer yourself—not a test question, a leading question, or a teaching question. Can you answer your own question in at least two different ways that are supported by the text?

**Share your curiosity and enthusiasm.** Lead with your curiosity, not your knowledge. By sharing what you are curious about and admitting what you don't know, you model the attitude you are asking students to adopt.

**Encourage students to think for themselves.** Try to remain in the role of leader by only asking questions. You should not answer questions or endorse ideas by making statements such as "Good idea" or, especially, "I agree" or "I disagree."

**Listen carefully and ask follow-up questions often.** Careful, attentive listening is the most important skill a Shared Inquiry leader can cultivate. Follow-up questions—spontaneous questions that arise from a leader's ability to listen closely and respond directly to students— drive and sustain an effective discussion. They help students develop their ideas and help everyone think more carefully about the relationships between different answers.

The best follow-up questions can be as simple as *Can you repeat that?* or *What made you think so?* Follow-up questions can

- **Clarify comments.** *What do you mean by that? Can you explain that another way?*

- **Get evidence.** *What in the poem gave you that idea? What did the character say or do that made you think so?*

- **Test and develop ideas.** *If you think that's what the character means, then why does this happen in the story? Is there anything in the story that doesn't seem to go with your answer?*

- **Elicit additional opinions.** *What do you think about what she just said? Do you agree with that idea? Does anyone have an idea we haven't heard yet?*

**Track student participation with a seating chart.** Keep track of discussion by marking which students participate and how. A check mark by a student's name can indicate that a student offered an answer, the notation "NA" can indicate that a student had no answer when asked to speak, and so on. The chart can help you identify patterns of participation in your class and evaluate students' contributions.

**Ask students to look back at the text frequently.** Asking students to find passages that support their answers helps everyone think about the specifics of the selection and keeps discussion on track. Revisiting the text and asking students to read portions aloud helps clear up misunderstandings and prompts new questions and interpretations. You might even go into discussion with a couple of passages in mind that you think are relevant to exploring your opening question.

**Return often to the opening question.** To keep discussion focused, ask students how their thoughts relate to the question you posed at the beginning of the discussion. This reminds everyone of the problem the group is trying to solve and helps students consider it in depth.

**Create opportunities for quieter students to speak.** It's easy for talkative students to dominate discussion, with quieter ones getting shut out. Marking participation on a seating chart can alert you to this pattern; if it happens in your group, try asking quieter students if they've heard an answer they agree with or what answer they wrote down on the Building Your Answer page.

**Encourage students to speak directly to one another.** If you address students by name and ask them to explain their ideas to one another, you will foster an environment of open inquiry and respect.

**End discussion when your group has discussed the opening question in depth.** You will usually be able to sense when your group has considered a number of answers to the opening question and most students could, if asked, provide their own "best answer" to the question. You may wish to check by asking *Are there any different ideas we haven't heard yet? Is there any part of the text we should look at before wrapping up?* Remind students that they will not reach consensus on an answer, because the selections support multiple interpretations. Having students complete the Building Your Answer page is an effective way to help them consider how discussion has changed or expanded their initial answers. If students seem eager to talk about ideas in the selection that relate to their own lives, you can use one of the Writing After Discussion prompts for discussion as a class or in small groups, as well as for writing.

**Periodically ask students to assess their work in discussion.** After every two or three discussions, ask students to share their thoughts on how discussion is going and how it might be improved. Help the class set specific goals for improvement in areas such as supporting their opinions with evidence from the text, staying focused on the meaning of the text under discussion, and speaking directly to other students rather than just to the leader.

# Building Your Answer in
# Shared Inquiry Discussion

Name: _____

Selection: _____

Your leader's opening question: _____

Your answer before discussion: _____

How did discussion affect your answer? Did it change your mind? Provide additional support for your answer?
Make you aware of additional issues? _____

_____

_____

_____

_____

Your answer after discussion: _____

_____

_____

_____

What in the selection helped you decide on this answer? _____

_____

## Writing After Discussion

- Gives students practice in systematically articulating, supporting, and developing their ideas

- Stimulates original thought and prompts students to connect what they read to their own experiences and opinions

- Helps students build a commitment to reading and critical thinking by continuing their thoughtful engagement with a selection's ideas

Because Shared Inquiry Discussion requires students to consider questions of meaning in depth, it is an excellent springboard to further exploring ideas through writing. Having students write an interpretive essay explaining and supporting the answer they developed on the Building Your Answer page is always an option for writing after discussion.

In addition, the Writing After Discussion prompts included in each unit give students opportunities to use different types of writing to connect the issues in a selection with their own experiences or to further explore the ideas raised by a selection. Although suggested as optional homework assignments, some of these topics can provide the basis for further classroom discussion.

# Vocabulary

The Perfection Learning student anthologies provide some short definitions of unfamiliar words as footnotes and a concept vocabulary at the beginning of the book. There are a number of other ways you can help students expand their vocabularies and learn strategies for understanding words that are new to them:

- Encourage students to raise questions about words they find unusual or confusing during the Sharing Questions session.

- Ask questions that guide students to search the context for clues to a word's meaning.

- Have students keep lists of new words that they find interesting, unusual, or helpful.

# Assessment

Whether or not you assign a grade for participation in Great Books, sharing your goals with students gives them a clear idea of what they are working toward, or what is expected of them, and helps them perform better. Evaluating students' progress and your own performance can also help you become a better leader, since there is a direct connection between what you do and the quality of discussion. Your choice of follow-up questions and willingness to listen will encourage students to develop their own ideas, support them with evidence from the text, and work together to explore the selection as a group. Progress as well as performance in reading, oral language, writing, and thinking skills should all be considered when you evaluate your students.

For the evaluation of oral work, your seating charts will provide a record of students' participation and the ideas they expressed in Shared Inquiry Discussion. Comparing these notes from week to week will help you give students feedback on their progress, individually or as a group.

A portfolio can show each student's improvements and strengths. When you collect students' written work, including the Building Your Answer page as well as any Writing After Discussion assignments, you might ask them for all of the work on one unit of their choice or from units covered both earlier and later in the semester. Let students select and evaluate some of their own pieces.

Students' ability to express themselves in writing is not always the same as their ability to express themselves in discussion. To promote critical thinking, focus on the content of what a student has written, rather than the mechanics. You can always have students work on mechanics during a revision stage.

Writing and assessment are covered in specialized consultation days offered as advanced professional development for leaders of Shared Inquiry Discussion. Call the Great Books Foundation at 1-800-222-5870 or visit www.greatbooks.org for more information about all of our professional development offerings and anthologies of literature.

# Discussion Unit 1

## The Typewriter

### Dorothy West

## Text Opener

Why do people often enjoy pretending to be someone else?

## Directed Notes

Mark places where the main character **accepts** reality with **A**, and places where he **escapes** reality with **E**.

## Interpretive Questions for Discussion

**Why is pretending to be J. Lucius Jones so important to the main character?**

1. Why does the main character hate everything in his life—"his flat and his family and his friends"—so much that he has "the insane desire to crush and kill"?

2. Why has the main character gone fifteen years without telling Net that he doesn't want to eat the same meal every Monday night?

3. Why does the main character think of the typewriter as "a vampire slowly drinking his blood"?

4. Why does the main character undergo a "chameleon change" once he starts dictating letters to Millie?

5. Why does the main character sign and mail the J. Lucius Jones letters? Why does he begin answering them?

6. Why does reading about J. P. Morgan in the silent sitting-room make the main character feel that it is "the end of everything"?

**Are we meant to think that the main character is responsible for creating the life he hates or that he is the victim of circumstances?**

1. Why doesn't West give the main character a name?

2. Why does the main character stay in Boston, even though he hates it?

3. Why doesn't the main character ever express his true feelings to Net and Mrs. Hicks?

4. When the main character is referred to as "not the progressive type," is this a justification that he makes to himself or a fact that the author tells us?

5. Why does West call Millie's request "the first of that series of great moments that every humble little middle-class man eventually experiences"?

6. Why does J. Lucius Jones crash and die at the end of the story?

7. Why does the main character hide from Millie how seriously he is taking the role of J. Lucius Jones?

## Writing After Discussion

1. Have you ever felt that you wanted to escape from your life? What did you do in order to cope?

2. Do daydreams help people achieve their ambitions or prevent people from achieving things?

3. What does a person need to feel in control of his or her life? What must a person do or have in order to feel powerful and not helpless?

4. Investigate the meaning of the word *progressive* as it was applied to African Americans during the first part of the twentieth century. What kinds of beliefs about the individual and society does this term express?

# DISCUSSION UNIT 2

## Any Human to Another

### COUNTEE CULLEN

## Text Opener

Are people more likely to be drawn together by a celebration or by a tragedy?

## Directed Notes

Mark places in the poem that emphasize **similarities** between people with **S**, and places that emphasize what is **distinct** about each person with **D**.

## Interpretive Questions for Discussion

**Is the speaker saying that the intertwining of "your grief and mine" is inevitable, or something that people should strive for?**

1. Why does the poem tell us that it is *any* human speaking?

2. How can the intertwining of grief be "diverse yet single"?

3. Why does the speaker say that the mingling of grief *must* happen?

4. In the last stanza, why does the speaker compare "your every grief" to a sword that strikes him down, but liken his own sorrow to a crown to be placed on the listener's head?

5. Is the speaker making a distinction between sorrow and grief?

**Is the speaker saying that grief must be shared but that joy can be kept to oneself?**

1. Why does the speaker say, "Joy may be shy, unique,/ Friendly to a few"? Who are the few to whom joy is friendly?

2. What does the "little tent/Pitched in a meadow" represent? Why is it a meadow of both "sun and shadow"?

3. Why does the speaker say that no one should be "so proud / And confident" to think that he is "allowed/A little tent"?

## Writing After Discussion

1. What does the speaker believe will result from the mingling of grief that he says must happen?

2. Is the speaker saying that we should empathize with the sorrow of all people, regardless of the reasons for that sorrow? Do you think this is possible or desirable?

3. Describe someone whom you dislike from what you imagine his or her point of view to be. Try to imagine and express how that person feels when he or she is unhappy and suffering.

4. Can empathy be taught? If you were a teacher or parent, how would you approach a child who seemed uncaring or unmoved by another student's distress?

# DISCUSSION UNIT 3

## How It Feels to Be Colored Me

ZORA NEALE HURSTON

## Text Opener

Write down ten words you would use to describe yourself.
(Leader, then ask: *Do any of the words you chose relate to your race or ethnicity? How important are these in defining who you are?*)

## Directed Notes

Mark places where Hurston suggests that her race is **important** to her with **I**, and places where she suggests that it is **not important** to her with **NI**.

## Interpretive Questions for Discussion

**Why is Hurston astonished rather than angry when she faces racial discrimination?**

1. What does Hurston make of the fact that the Northern visitors to Eatonville wanted to see her sing and dance, while the "colored people" deplored her "joyful tendencies"?

2. How does Hurston feel about having been "everybody's Zora"?

3. Does Hurston think of having become "colored" as a positive or a negative thing?

4. What does Hurston mean when she says that she became "a little colored girl" in her "heart as well as in the mirror"?

5. According to Hurston, what does it mean to be "tragically colored"?

6. What does Hurston mean when she says that "the world is to the strong regardless of a little pigmentation more or less"?

7. Why does Hurston describe herself as not weeping at the world because "I am too busy sharpening my oyster knife"?

8. Why does Hurston use the story about listening to music at the jazz club to explain when her "color comes"?

9. Why does Hurston have "no separate feeling about being an American citizen and colored"?

## How significant does Hurston believe the differences are between black and white people?

1. When Hurston describes moving from Eatonville to Jacksonville, why does she say that she "suffered a sea change"?

2. Why does Hurston say that "for any act of mine, I shall get twice as much praise or twice as much blame"?

3. Why does Hurston maintain that the position of her "white neighbor" is much more difficult than hers and that being black is "exciting"? Is she being serious or sarcastic?

4. Why does Hurston compare herself to a dark rock being covered by the tide when she is surrounded by white people?

5. How does Hurston feel about the contrast between herself and her white friend at the jazz concert when she says that "he is so pale with his whiteness then and I am so colored"?

6. When Hurston says that "at certain times I have no race, I am me," does she mean that to be aware of her race is not to be fully herself?

7. Why does Hurston compare people to bags filled with "miscellany"? Why does she say that if the bags were emptied "all might be dumped in a single heap and the bags refilled without altering the content of any greatly"? Why does Hurston suggest that this is how the "Great Stuffer of Bags" might have created people in the first place?

## Writing After Discussion

1. Do you agree with Hurston's image of people as differently colored bags with randomly distributed contents? Is it possible to make any accurate generalizations about what people are like on the basis of race?

2. Consider a label that has been placed on you or a friend (for example, "jock," "gifted," "learning disabled"). How do you feel about this label? When are you aware of it and when do you forget about it? Explore these questions about identity in an essay.

3. Do you agree with Hurston that "the world is to the strong regardless of a little pigmentation"?

4. Is Hurston correct when she says of slavery that "the operation was successful and the patient is doing well"? Do you think it is better to remember slavery in America or to forget it?

# DISCUSSION UNIT 4

## The Pink Hat

### CAROLINE BOND DAY

## Text Opener

If you could get into an exclusive club only by concealing something about yourself, would you do it?

## Directed Notes

Mark places where the narrator seems **confident** with **C**, and places where she seems **uncomfortable** with **U**.

## Interpretive Questions for Discussion

**Does the narrator regret having used the pink hat to pass as a white person?**

1. Why does the narrator describe her hat as if it were magic, an "enchanted cloak" and "Aladdin's lamp"?

2. Does the narrator tell us that the teaching profession is "exhausting" and that her life is "periodically flat" so that we'll admire her or excuse her?

3. Once she realizes that she has been mistaken for a white woman while wearing the hat, why does the narrator decide "to experiment further"?

4. Why does the narrator tell us that "starvation of body or soul sometimes breeds criminals"?

5. Does the narrator "deliberately set out to deceive" because she is curious or because she finds it thrilling?

6. Why does the narrator feel that she "could not have borne the questioning eyes of the colored waiters" at restaurants?

7. Why does the narrator describe the white people at the art shows as "really nice, likable folk too, when they don't know one"?

8. Why does the narrator experience "a crash" after the Greek play?

9. At the end of the story, is the narrator being sincere or ironic when she tells us, "My spirit has knit together as well as my bones"?

## Writing After Discussion

1. Do you think what the narrator did was justified? Would you have done it in her place?

2. If you were in the narrator's position, could you be content at the end of the story?

3. The narrator tells us that she is "a mulatto—anthropologically speaking. I am a dominant of the white type of the F3 generation of secondary crossings." Investigate how "blackness" was defined for legal purposes during the period when racial segregation was enforced in the United States. (See especially the 1896 Supreme Court case *Plessy v. Ferguson*.)

# DISCUSSION UNIT 5

## The Negro Artist and the Racial Mountain

### LANGSTON HUGHES

## Text Opener

If you were telling the story of your life, how significant would your racial or ethnic background be?

## Directed Notes

Mark places where Hughes describes **barriers** that prevent a black artist from being himself with **B.**

## Interpretive Questions for Discussion

**According to Hughes, who or what is responsible for the racial mountain?**

1. Does Hughes see the racial mountain more as a barrier to black artists' achievements or as a means to their fulfillment?

2. Why does Hughes say that the young poet's "desire to run away spiritually from his race" will prevent him from being a "great poet"?

3. According to Hughes, where does the "urge within the race toward whiteness" come from?

4. Why does Hughes believe that it is so important for black artists to resist pouring their "racial individuality into the mold of American standardization"?

5. Is Hughes saying that there is an opposition for the black artist between being black and being American?

6. Why does Hughes think that it is so difficult for a would-be artist from a middle-class black family to interpret "the beauty of his own people"?

7. Why does Hughes believe that the "vogue in things Negro . . . may do as much harm as good for the budding colored artist"?

8. What are the "unintentional bribes from the whites" that the black artist must work against?

9. Why does Hughes say, at the end of his essay, that if black people are not pleased, "their displeasure doesn't matter," when earlier he criticizes black people who do not embrace the works of black artists?

**Is Hughes being restrictive or encouraging when he explains what he believes to be the "duty of the younger Negro artist"?**

1. According to Hughes, what makes someone a "great poet"?

2. Why does Hughes think that the black artist must be closer to "the low-down folks, the so-called common element" to create authentic black art?

3. Why does Hughes emphasize that the black artist can help his people "catch a glimmer of their own beauty"?

4. How does Hughes think a black artist can tell whether he is choosing his subject freely or out of fear?

5. Why is Hughes "ashamed for" the black artist who doesn't choose black subjects for his art?

## Writing After Discussion

1. If a black artist's work is embraced and even copied by white people, does it cease to be black art? Has anything changed in the worlds of art, music, and literature since Hughes wrote this essay?

2. Do artists have a greater responsibility to themselves or to society? Which artists do you know of who exemplify this responsibility?

3. Think of a work of art—a book, a painting, a song—that is meaningful to you. Write about what makes it important to you and to what extent the artist's background and the subject of the work are similar to your own background.

# Discussion Unit 6

## Miss Cynthie

### Rudolph Fisher

## Text Opener

What would you do if you were proud of accomplishing something that you thought your parents might not approve of?

## Directed Notes

Mark places where Miss Cynthie **approves** of something with **A,** and places where she **disapproves** of something with **D.**

## Interpretive Questions for Discussion

**What makes Miss Cynthie change her mind about David's career?**

1. Why has David told his grandmother that he wouldn't ever be happy until she came to see " 'zackly what he was doin' " in New York?

2. Why is David confident that Miss Cynthie's ideas can be changed?

3. Why does Miss Cynthie continually look at the audience in the theater to see their expressions?

4. What is the "blend of truth and novelty" that captures Miss Cynthie's attention during the first scene at the theater?

5. Why does Miss Cynthie assume that "not one" of the audience "knew or cared to know the loving kindness of God"?

6. Why does seeing the theater audience as a "crowd of children" make Miss Cynthie reassess David's career?

7. Why are we told at the end of the story that Miss Cynthie was perhaps thinking "God moves in a mysterious way," while mouthing the words to a song?

**Why does David believe that Miss Cynthie is "really responsible for [his] success"?**

1. Why does David tell Miss Cynthie, "Tomorrow night you'll know the worst," before taking her to the theater?

2. Why does riding in David's fast car impress Miss Cynthie so much?

3. Why does David take Miss Cynthie to Harlem?

4. Why does David tell Ruth to listen as Miss Cynthie softly sings the song about "the gal with the hole in her stockin' "?

5. Why does Miss Cynthie suddenly see David's act as "the guileless antics" of a child?

6. Does David think that he has followed Miss Cynthie's advice to "do like a church steeple—aim high and go straight"?

7. Why won't Miss Cynthie take more than a leaf when David offers her the flower?

## Writing After Discussion

1. Do you agree with Miss Cynthie when she says that "places is pretty much alike after people been in 'em awhile"? What is she saying people do to make all places alike?

2. Do children tend to live out the dreams and ambitions their parents have for them? Is it always obvious when children are or are not living them out?

3. Should parents or other relatives tell children what career they wish them to choose?

# TITLES OF RELATED INTEREST FROM THE GREAT BOOKS FOUNDATION

The Great Books Foundation publishes the following readings on related topics, along with interpretive questions for discussion, note-taking suggestions, and writing activities. *Modern American Poetry, Reader's Guide to* The Great Gatsby, and *The Will of the People: Readings in American Democracy* are available for purchase on our Web site or by calling 1-800-222-5870.

### *Modern American Poetry*

This anthology, which begins with Walt Whitman, expresses the range and vigor of modern American poetry and offers a practical approach to reading and discussing it. It includes a brief biography of Langston Hughes and seven of his best-loved poems, as well as the work of other African American poets.

### *Reader's Guide to* The Great Gatsby

F. Scott Fitzgerald's masterpiece is set in the Jazz Age, the same period as the Harlem Renaissance. Gatsby, like the main character in Dorothy West's story, "The Typewriter," is caught up in the American dream of self-invention, playing a game that he eventually loses. This collection of resources for reading and discussion includes interpretive questions and passages for close reading, writing suggestions, and letters and a short story by Fitzgerald. The text of the novel is not included. Background and context pieces include photographs and selected documents from and about the 1920s on Prohibition, flappers, jazz, and the spirit of the age.

**_The Will of the People: Readings in American Democracy_**
This collection of fundamental documents in American history includes the poem "Let America Be America Again" by Langston Hughes. "O, yes, / I say it plain, / America never was America to me, / And yet I swear this oath— / America will be!"